tagbook
the bolt® book of questions and answers

tagbook™
the bolt® book of questions and answers

Edited by
Kate Levitt and Dennis Sarkozy
with
Michael Gartland, Ari Voukydis, and Elizabeth Hurchalla

THREE RIVERS PRESS
NEW YORK

BOLT® and 🅱️®️ are registered service marks of Bolt, Inc.
TAGBOOKS™, BOLTEVERYWHERE™ and related logos and
characters are trademarks and service marks owned by Bolt, Inc.

Published by Three Rivers Press, New York, New York.
Member of the Crown Publishing Group.

Random House, Inc. New York, Toronto, London, Sydney, Auckland
www.randomhouse.com

THREE RIVERS PRESS is a registered trademark and the Three
Rivers Press colophon is a trademark of Random House, Inc.

Printed in the United States of America

Design by Lane Vandeventer

Library of Congress Cataloging-in-Publication Data is available upon
request.

ISBN 0-609-80805-2

10 9 8 7 6 5 4 3 2 1

First Edition

The questions and answers in this book were provided by Bolt members
and do not necessarily reflect the thoughts or opinions of Bolt, Inc.

Foreword

Just because you're talking doesn't mean people hear what you're saying. And just because there are a lot of places to carry on a conversation doesn't mean that all of them feel real. Sometimes, though, you find a place where you can ask any question and create the environment you want.

The two of us found exactly that kind of place for totally different reasons: One of us wanted a place to make fun of poser punks and meet straight-edge vegan hardcore kids, and one of us was trying to find other politically active B-girls. Even though we were searching for completely different things, we both found what we were looking for on Bolt.

Bolt thrives on people thriving on each other. If the Glee Club just isn't doing it for you at the moment, where can you turn? Cults aren't the answer, and neither is binge gas-huffing. All those TV shows and teen magazines that offer advice aren't the answer, either. That's why Bolt started online Tagbooks—to let members ask whatever questions they want and hear what other people really think. Sometimes the questions are silly, sometimes they're serious and provocative. Either way, they're straight from the source—uncensored and unrestricted.

Until now, you could only access Tagbook questions online, and answering them was a solitary activity. This book brings Tagbooks out into the real world, where you can use them to get a glimpse into your own or someone else's brain. The questions in this book are fun to read and even better for meeting and getting to know people. Use them as icebreakers when you're on a date and the conversation's drying up. Or when you're waiting in line for a show, bored in class, on a long road trip, or just looking for some uninhibited responses at a party.

Here's one: What's the biggest lie you've ever told? How would you answer? How would your best friend answer? How would the pizza delivery guy answer? Whatever it is, the reply will tell you something about the person you're asking.

You've always wondered what was going on in the minds of the people you see every day. Now's your chance to ask.

Kate Levitt (Bolt name: kwalaty)
Dennis Sarkozy (Bolt name: ruse)

P.S. Want to record your answer to one of the questions inside? Want to find out more about a Bolt member whose question or answer is featured here? Just go to www.bolt.com/tagbook. Once there, you can also create questions of your own—and maybe your question will be in the next print edition of *Tagbook*!

Acknowledgements

This book would have been impossible without the members of Bolt (and especially big ups to the those whose questions and answers appear within). More than anyone else, we thank them for making it all happen just by being themselves.

We'd also like to thank everyone who put in countless hours and stayed up late nights to drop this gem. *Tagbook* would still be a gleam in our eyes if it weren't for the following people: AJ, David Balfour, Big T, Stacie Billis, Josh Borock, Erika Boudreau-Harris, Megan Brenn-White, Elvin Can, Jake Daniel, Cameron Dardis, Cierra Dardis, Emily Dignan, Duerte and Bonnie, Jen Emery, Rebecca Federman, Michelle Finocchi, Aron Galonsky, Adam Gartland, Alice Gartland, Denis Gartland, Diane Goodman, Kevin Gould, Daniel Greenberg, Michael Gwertzman, Annie Hall, Mary Ho, Jessica Hulett, Jeff Jarrett, J-Lai, Steve Kamen, Paul Kekalos, Rob Kingston, Doris Kirschenbaum, Morris Kirschenbaum, Rachel Kleinman, Yael Kropsky, Michael Liss, Dan Malanga, Jennifer Mangali, Bob Mecoy, Michael Merrill, Michelle Morrissey, Jane Mount, Myke Myers, Jason Ojalvo, Peter Olson, Philip Patrick, Jase Patrizio, Dan Pelson, Amanda Peters, Blake Radcliffe, Hafeez Raji, Roshot, Cathy Sarkozy, Steve Sarkozy, Sam Schechner, Jason Schneider, Gordon Shumway, Dorianne Steele, Robyn Steinhause, the SoD kids, Lane Vandeventer, Inga Veksler, Leah Weatherspoon, James Wood, Alyssa Zygmunt, and the entire Bolt staff.

Finally, an extra special shout-out goes to Bolt copy editor Robert "Dreamy" Buscemi for his tenacity, wit, and editing superpowers.

With much love and respect, thank you.

your body, yourself, your precious feelings

What is your favorite way to be a pain in the butt?

Lizardchica
18/F/United States

Q

A

Asking guys if they'll make out in front of me.

Sykedelic84
16/F/United States

I like to sit in a lawn chair in my front yard with a hair dryer and pretend to shoot passing motorists.

agentorange3188
18/F/United States

What terrifies you?

nilomeca
20/M/United States

Q

A

My biggest fear in life is having my eye poked out. I know that sounds weird, but it's the truth. If I am walking through the woods at night, I usually put my hands around my eyes so some branch doesn't poke one of them out.

starrbryt
18/F/United States

Things touching my face (especially spiderwebs) and anything that crawls.

high_current
23/M/United States

What's the easiest way to piss you off?

the_chick2000
17/F/United Kingdom

Q

A

Get into an argument with me and dismiss my comments by saying "whatever."

super-vixxxen
17/F/United States

Imitate my voice or my laugh.

writer_chic_15
16/F/Canada

Be annoyingly optimistic and perky.

Blood_thorns
20/F/Canada

Hit me on the head with a large shovel.

poshkate
15/M/Vietnam

Put up one of those pig magnets that oink every time you open the refrigerator door.

kerplunk05
15/F/United States

Be fake.

sk8erkatie
15/F/United States

If you could undo one mistake, what would it be and why?

smallbear_00
F/16/United States

Q

A

Losing my virginity. I should have waited.

purplechick1221
17/F/United States

When my best friend told me a big secret, I went and told this guy with a huge mouth. I feel really bad because I know she doesn't completely trust me anymore.

shadysgirl1874
17/F/United States

I'd go back two years and not get caught stealing. I just now got off probation.

Dragon321
18/M/United States

If you could be with anyone in the world for a night, who would it be and why? What would you do?

Amazing_blonde
18/F/United States

Q

Steve Jobs, because he's brilliant and gorgeous. I'd talk with him for hours and have him give me inside info on new Apple products.

Lordess_Spleen
17/F/United States

My grandmother. She passed away when I was 15, and I love her with all my heart. I would tell her about my life and why I've done the things I've done. I'd ask for her forgiveness and her advice. And for a big hug.

LaQuila_Tequila
18/F/United States

Prince William, because I'd love to corrupt that nice little boy the royals raised!

emmy_elle
15/F/United States

What's the weirdest thing you've done in the shower?

□ Brushed your teeth
□ Peed
□ Sang a Britney Spears song
□ Shaved your legs
□ Done something nasty
□ Other

evilPOP_TART
15/F/United States

Q

A

Brushed your teeth: 14%
Peed: 11%
Sang a Britney Spears song: 18%
Shaved your legs: 1%
Done something nasty: 53%
Other: 3%

I made out with the shower wall so I could have a tester before I saw my boyfriend that day!

whit56
15/F/United States

Picked open a scab on my arm and wrote my name on the wall in blood. I think I was bored. . . .

depressedkitten
17/M/United States

I was listening to Rob Zombie and head-banging, and I hit my head on the marble wall.

hangemhigh
16/M/United States

If you could be a member of the opposite sex for a day, what would you do first?

DreamWriterGurl
18/F/United States

Q

Drink milk out of the carton.

Cavina
15/F/United States

I would stay a girl . . . it may be tough sometimes, but girls have WAY more fun!

FlirtyBuck
16/F/United States

A

Seduce this really hot gay friend I have.

da__chick
20/F/United States

I'd definitely stay a guy. I love girls, but I feel bad for them. Girls have to deal with so much more than guys. When I'm out for a long bike ride or running I can just jump in the bushes and take a piss. And girls have to put up with guys who only want them for sex.

electronicparty
20/M/United States

1. Moan about how big my thighs look
2. Go shopping
3. Experience a period
4. Spend three hours getting ready to go out
5. Realize I was better off male and watch the clock!

virtua69
20/M/England

If you were invisible, what would you do?

Bohemia
17/F/United Kingdom

Q

A

I would walk around pinching everybody's butts.

Kristyn28
18/F/United States

I'd stand next to my old headmaster and fart all day.

Leek
19/M/Wales

You know how people say "The last thing I need is . . ."? Well, what IS the last thing you need?

BLaCkSuNsEt
16/F/United States

Q

A

A stalker.

iokua_surfboy
19/M/United States

To go back into a really deep depression again—I had two rounds of it already this year and God knows I don't need another.

Soopydear
16/F/Canada

For my brother to have another bean burrito. I still remember the last time— that's why I've since invested in a gas mask.

crazy_chick2343
15/F/United States

What are you most self-conscious about?

curley1120
17/F/United States

Q

My voice. Some people say it's cute, but others say it's "different." It's small and kinda squeaky. But I never tell anyone that I'm self-conscious about it because I'm afraid it will draw more attention to it.

littleamy
18/F/United States

Saying the wrong thing at the wrong time and looking like a total ass.

mxpxpunkgurl
17/F/United States

If you could choose to either never be sick again or never be sad again, which would it be?

jamie003
19/F/United States

Q

A

I would choose to never be sad again, because if I were happy and loved and puking my guts out, I would be better off than if I were sad and depressed and healthy.

silverjbullet
19/F/Canada

Never to be sick again, 'cause being sad is a part of life, whereas being sick just brings down your life. You can learn from being sad. You can die from being sick.

Schmiddy_sr
15/M/Canada

I would choose to never be sick again because sadness is sort of refreshing in a way—sometimes you need to just cry to a friend or into your pillow and let it all out. . . . It helps me a lot and then I feel a lot better.

SoooBlonde
16/F/United States

Name one thing that most people don't know about you.

punkgirl2960
17/F/United States

Q

A

I like writing stories and poetry, and I'm actually a thoughtful person. Everyone thinks I'm wild and outgoing and loud. . . .

Beachbabe2412
16/F/Australia

I have colon cancer. I am going to get it cut out if possible, so I am not telling anyone unless I have to.

Stacy785
16/F/United States

I'm not really that deep. I can be, but I'd just like to take a break and not be seen as an egghead.

izzknot
16/M/United States

Do you have a recurring dream?

AvalonAyla
18/F/United States

A

Ever since I was a little kid, I've been having the same damn dream. I'm sitting in an army tank opening bags and bags of marshmallows.

Stroke9er
15/F/United States

I have these dreams where I see things that happen the next day. Like I'll see my mom or friend do something in my dream, then the next day, it will happen exactly like it did in the dream. It's freaky.

QTPie47
15/F/United States

I'm on a beautiful beach and I spend the whole time playing in the ocean. Always the same beach, beach house, friends, everything. I love it. Then I wake up to North Texas.

JBParrot1013
15/F/United States

Do you ever hate yourself? What do you do about it?

dabighabib
17/M/United States

Q

A

I hate being myself every week when I switch from my mom's house to my dad's and vice versa. I write poetry or call my friends, or just think of all the positive things about myself.

chellyrayrach
15/F/United States

Sometimes. When that happens I usually go nuts and kick things and jump around in circles and yell to let out some of the rage I feel toward myself.

lotus4201
18/F/United States

If you were psychic, what would you do with your powers?

sweetcherry1
15/F/United States

Q

A

I would use my powers to actually pass a geometry test.

d_last_disciple
15/M/United States

I would look at every guy and see if he was a pig or a gentleman.

katiescarlett5
17/F/United States

I'd know all the lotto numbers and win millions!

PlaStyKa
20/F/Canada

What's your favorite word?

sandgirl666
15/F/United Kingdom

Q

A

"Hemoglobin."

ManicLise
18/F/United States

"Cacophony."

Klothos
18/F/United States

"Limes." It just feels cool when you say it.

Monotonelime
17/F/United States

I say "disgruntle" a lot.

LCStarry
15/F/United States

It's a tie between "squirrel" and "sleet."

PrinCeSsShAwNa
15/F/United States

What makes you a badass?

PureK
18/F/United States

Q

A

There's not a rule I haven't broken, not a single mall cop who hasn't yelled at me.

ThePixieQueen
15/F/United States

I'm three vertebrae short of a complete spine.

oOPEZOo
17/M/United States

I've pulled a tree out of the ground with my hands and wrestled a horse to the ground.

noosedaddy
19/M/United States

What's your most prized possession?

**yankeegirl02
18/F/United States**

Q

A

My Koran.

yaz4jules
18/F/United Kingdom

A little book my best friend made for me the last night of our freshman year in college. It had all of the funny things we'd said throughout the entire year in it.

Angelbaby6671
21/F/United States

My neon-blue, snake-print boots. They go everywhere with me.

heartlesschick
20/F/Canada

My backpack of journals. I've had them forever—the first one was from when I was in third grade.

Im_Just_Strange
15/F/Canada

What is the safest place you know?

your_destiny
20/F/United States

Q

A

A mosh pit at a good punk show.

mynthe
15/F/United States

Belize. It is a tropical haven where people can relax—and the crazier you act, the more people will like you.

Greg_Andrew
17/M/Belize

This may sound weird, but my safest spot is my German class in school. I like to stay there during study hall and lunch and talk to this guy I like who stays there too. I'm totally myself there, and it's just a nice place to sit and think and speak your mind.

ybagirl
16/F/United States

Underneath the sink. With a blanket.

smallpoet
17/F/United States

What's the freakiest thing you've ever done in public?

DymeLikeWhoa464
15/F/United States

A

I had sex on the courthouse lawn under a big tree in the front of the building. It was great until me and my girlfriend got caught by a judge.

Jgowan
23/M/United States

I sang "God Must Have Spent a Little More Time on You" over the school PA system for my girlfriend just after the principal finished the morning announcements. She was totally embarrassed, but she liked it.

porno_fan
18/M/United States

At McDonald's there was this really cute guy at the register, so my buds dared me to go up there and yell out, "No, I will NOT sleep with you for a Happy Meal! Please quit using your status to get women!" The whole place looked over at him and he turned beet red.

Gummie_bears_00
15/F/Canada

people, places, and things that piss you off

Name one thing you wish your parents knew about you, but you can't bring yourself to tell them.

angel12082
18/F/United States

Q

A

I want my dad to understand that I'm not the best at everything I do. I'm not always first to answer and I'm not always the fastest swimmer or the fastest hurdler.

LaurenShojo
16/F/United States

I'm a Wiccan and my parents are Christian. I can't tell them, but I want to.

sagagrl
17/F/Netherlands

I wish I could tell my dad and grandparents I love them, but I haven't talked to them in about four years and am kinda afraid to call. Last time we spoke I told them to go to hell and that I never wanted to talk to them again.

nightwolf72
21/M/United States

I want them to know that I am still really, really bummed about their divorce, which happened five years ago.

Danie_jb4115
17/F/United States

***What's the worst thing your parents ever
found out about you?***

***RainbowGurl7707
18/F/United States***

Q

A

My mom found out I was raped by my best friend's 18-year-old boyfriend. I was only 12. I thought she would never get over it.

jjc0377
23/F/United States

That I had a son for two years before my mom found out.

porno_fan
18/M/United States

Tell me one thing you love and one thing you hate about the place you live.

superkitty
20/F/United States

Q

A

Love: nothing. Hate: everything. There's nothing to do. All the people are on drugs and/or stink so bad you can't get near them. Our school is in debt $750,000, all our sports teams suck, a ton of teachers quit last year and they still haven't had any applications for some of the positions, and there is NOTHING TO DO! I live in Hicksville, USA.

> *bite_my_butt*
> *15/F/United States*

Hate: I live in a very small town in Texas and there isn't much in the way of civilization. The schools are small so you can only have a few friends. Love: It's a peaceful county with plenty of room for my horses to graze when their colts are born! Plus all of my friends are crazy and I love them to death.

> *butterflykixass*
> *17/F/United States*

I love the fact that there's no crime. What I hate is people walking over our lawn.

> *anzac*
> *15/M/Australia*

How do you feel when people use the word "gay" as a generic insult?

mizuonna
18/F/Japan

Q

A

I have to admit I'm guilty of using that term, but I try hard not to. I have a gay family member, so I feel REALLY bad when I use it. Another word I use that I wish that I didn't is "retarded." I HATE that I say that!

Dacia_Vu
16/F/United States

I have absolutely nothing against gay people. I have aunts and uncles who are gay, so I've grown up around it and am pretty comfortable about it. I use "gay" as an insult a lot, but I don't really think of it as having the same meaning. I don't mean it as rude and my friends don't either; it's just something stupid we say.

poster_girl
15/F/United States

*If you could vote anyone off the planet,
who would it be and why?*

Q

*StreetPunk007
17/M/United States*

Greedy corporate execs who are mistreating the poverty-stricken and destroying the environment.

Lizardchica
18/F/United States

A

On a local level, this guy Bryan who sleeps with jailbait and tells them all he loves them then dumps them . . . including my best friend. On a global level, Dr. Laura . . . she's a poser bigot.

Chasing_Sirens
18/F/United States

OPEC, Britney Spears, all boy bands and all the factories where they are manufactured.

psplayer
20/M/Canada

Puff Daddy or Tony Blair—I hate them both equally.

twiggyramirez99
16/M/United Kingdom

If they were going somewhere cool, I'd vote for myself.

amongtheflames
17/F/Canada

If you had to live with only one of your parents, which one would you choose and why?

☐ *Mom*
☐ *Dad*
☐ *Neither*
☐ *Grandparents*

amberlou62
18/F/United States

Q

A

Mom: 53%
Dad: 25%
Neither: 19%
Grandparents: 3%

Neither. It may seem odd, but I would choose my stepmom. She's always been there for me. She is patient and understanding and can answer all those girly questions. She made growing up much easier for me.

delekatala
19/F/United States

What if you found out the family you grew up with was not your biological family?

underdawg67
19/M/United Kingdom

Q

A

I'd be pissed that they kept it from me. Not surprised, though—my parents always drop weird bombshells on me like that.

peacefrog666
17/F/United States

Well, I would try to find my biological parents, but only to thank them for giving me the family that I have now.

wrpd24474
19/F/United States

Try to figure out why I look like both my parents.

Katty6763
21/F/United States

What do you think the spookiest everyday, common object is?

ruse
17/M/United States

Q

A

The eyelash curler. It's very helpful, yet it can also be a weapon.

twiggyeam21
16/F/United States

The watercooler. I hate the little "bloop-bloop-bloop" noises it makes at night.

LilyBliss
17/F/Canada

Who is the weirdest person you know?

bitch_20002001
16/F/United States

Q

A

My friend Daniel. For some strange reason, he always has something to say about his love of cheese!

lilprep2145
15/F/United States

A lot of people tell me that I am the weirdest kid they know. It might be that I can do almost 35 different voices, or that I wear a foam helmet and scream at people from my car. I still eat paste.

kiss7700
16/M/United States

I know a lot of weird people, but Clive is the worst. For starters, he is a Communist and he talks about crap I have never heard of: Khrushchev, Mao, etc. Also, he is totally obsessed with Garfield.

Super_SlimShady
15/M/United States

What is the most disgusting part of the human anatomy?

lost_etc
21/F/United States

Q

A

I don't get why guys stare at girls' butts. Why?! Don't they know what butts do?! Eww.

rollinsgrl1
18/F/United States

Do your parents pressure you to do things you don't want to do?

PrincessWillow
15/F/United States

A

Definitely! They've always had really high expectations—they're the kind of parents who say "What? An A-minus? Why isn't this an A-plus?" It gets irritating because I can never totally please them.

raffi00
18/F/United States

Yes, sometimes. It really helps when you move away to college, though. You do your homework and do good in school 'cause that's what they want, and they pay for you to go to college 'cause that's what you want.

santacruzchic
18/F/United States

What's the nicest thing anyone has ever done for you?

Sweetych
18/F/United States

Q

A

The guy who I was partnered with in the three-legged race in gym didn't say anything mean to me even though none of the guys like me.

clarinetgirl33
17/F/United States

When my boyfriend put wildflowers all over the inside of my car while I was at school.

Flower_Child777
16/F/United States

I was at a party once and got into this argument with some girl. Someone I didn't even know came up behind me, bitched her out, and totally stood up for me.

ecstasy18
18/F/United States

How would you react if you walked in on one of your parents cheating on the other?

Bunnie2K4
16/F/United States

Q

A

I hate my dad, so I wouldn't care if my mom cheated on him. But I would black out if he cheated on my mother, even though she might be happy to have a reason to kick him out!

diamonds190
16/F/United States

I wouldn't want to see either of my parents having sex no matter who it was with.

miss_kitty666
15/F/United States

Ask for money to keep it hush-hush. After all, this is America and we are a capitalist country.

dre_chronic
16/M/United States

What is the worst thing that our society accepts?

MeanSue
17/F/United States

Q

A

Carnies with big hands.

DjBoberus
18/M/United States

Stereotypes and people in positions of power. We base importance on employment, and that's just sad. My job does not reflect me, and I am certainly not my job. Society needs to do some growing up.

no_frills
17/F/Canada

Discrimination. I'm not just talking women or races—everyone. People are discriminated against because of their religion, sexual orientation, their hair color, everything. It's so screwed up.

halcy1
17/F/United States

Premarital sex and live-in boyfriends and girlfriends, especially among teenagers. Jeez, we're all going to hell!

EatAtMcDs4Free
15/F/United States

Who's somebody (famous or not) who really pisses you off? What do they do to make you so mad?

QueenSally
16/F/United States

Q

A

Well, there is this guy who has pissed me off ever since fourth grade. But the worst thing he ever did was in our ninth grade English class. I say what's on my mind and think of some pretty interesting things. I was having a good time in this class, sharing opinions and stuff, and since this boy doesn't understand some things I say, he decides they're stupid. He started taking bets with people in my class over how many "stupid" things I'd say in a class period. Every time I said something, I could hear him, two rows back: "There's one . . . there's two. . . ." Once I figured out what was going on, I was too mortified to say anything for the rest of the semester. But I did pound the little nerd into the ground the first chance I got.

koldblufyre
16/F/United States

I hate those freakin' Old Navy, Gap, and Calvin Klein commercials. The people on them make me want to go postal.

everloser
18/M/United States

You are an alien living unnoticed among Earthlings. When you report back to your planet, what will you say is the STRANGEST thing you witnessed during your stay?

Godowar
20/M/United States

A

Tofu.

yiloa
16/F/United States

The fact that some Earthlings have billions of dollars while others make less than $500 a year for doing backbreaking work.

martenique
20/F/United States

The faces people make during sex.

austin15
16/M/United States

It would have to be humans driving these deadly machines (cars) down the street with a cell phone and cigarette (also deadly) in one hand, a cup of coffee and a doughnut in the other hand, steering with their elbows.

Ppiew11
15/F/United States

*If you were going to have a revolution,
what kind of society would you create?*

Q

Light__Bringer
19/M/United States

A

One where everyone would get a fair share of what they deserve, and where the little guys would be more appreciated. Spreadin' the love equally is what it's all about.

Deejayegypto
20/M/United States

As close to a true democracy as is realistically feasible. Ideally, my revolution would change the values of a society in which $600,000 is spent on a car commercial while teachers take second jobs in pizza shops to pay the rent.

Saecha
22/F/United States

working for the man

If you had the power to institute a mandatory class in every high school in the world, what would the subject be?

Josh_the_great
19/M/United States

Q

A

Religions of the World 101. To teach about the beliefs of many different religions—not preach, teach.

WyNNeTH
21/M/United States

The class would be called "Haters 101," and only playa-hatas would have to take it. This class would teach others not to hate on someone just because they look, dress, talk, or act better than you.

KATINA69
18/F/United States

A free period off campus to go out to lunch and have fun!

SoooBlonde
16/F/United States

What is the worst or the weirdest thing that ever happened at school?

jpstf
16/M/Canada

Q

When a guy grabbed my butt, pulled me over, and then kissed me. He was my best friend at the time and apparently wanted to show me that he cared about me. I showed my feelings by giving him a black eye. I already had a boyfriend!

sporty1331
16/F/United States

A

I went schiz at one guy because he pegged a carrot and hit me in the eye.

MissPessimistic
17/F/Australia

I was wearing a padded bra in school and some padding fell onto the floor.

SexyCourtney
18/F/United States

There was this one guy who threatened to come to eighth grade graduation with a gun to get rid of his girlfriend; then there was the bomb threat, which had all of us scared out of our wits. They both sucked somewhat big time.

Kain550
16/M/United States

At a college party, this guy was messing around on the balcony, fell, and broke his legs. We thought it was funny, but when we got down there, we saw the bone had poked through his skin.

Amber95801
17/F/United States

Would you ever have sex with one of your teachers? Why or why not?

underdawg67
19/M/United States

Q

A

How do you think I'm passing Microeconomics?

Sweet_Hone_Bee
17/F/United States

If school were optional, would you go?
Why or why not?

Apekop83
16/F/Netherlands

Q

A

There are days when I'd definitely answer no, but I would feel so guilty for letting my mind waste away that I'd eventually go again.

Adriana_82
18/F/United States

Yeah, but I'd probably sleep in a lot. I'd go to see my friends and to learn.

starmegs
18/F/United States

Probably. I would be pretty bored at home. Plus I want to be edumacated.

FairieTale710
18/F/United States

If you were in class and someone said, "I hate preps—I wish I could kill them all," what would you do?

AE_fly_guy
15/M/United States

Q

A

How many times have you said, "I'm gonna kill so-and-so"? Did you actually do it?

vampirespike
17/M/United States

Yeah, like a prep has never said the same thing about goths! But if I ever heard anything like that from any kind of clique member, I'd tell them off. If I thought they were serious, I'd tell a teacher.

fireflame417
15/F/United States

I'd probably laugh and say, "Oh, that's so two years ago."

amongtheflames
17/F/Canada

What wouldn't you do for 10 million dollars?

greenapplz
21/F/United States

Q

A

I would never eat dog shit, camel shit, human shit, cat shit, fish shit, turtle shit, cow shit, duck shit, elephant shit, rat shit, mouse shit, zebra shit, flamingo shit, monkey shit, donkey shit, seal shit, bird shit, or any sort of shit for any amount of money. That would be so disgusting.

RioTdoll
16/F/United States

The only things that I wouldn't do are the big illegal things—like sell drugs or kill someone. Everything else is cool for 10 million.

fireofstars
16/F/United States

What's the grossest thing that you would do for money?

meza14
15/F/Canada

Q

A

Have sex in garbage.

greeneyes7482
17/F/United States

Lie in a bath filled with slime.

f007_wy
17/F/United States

What do you have to do even though it's definitely not in your job description?

QueridoTesoro
17/F/United States

Q

A

Hello! I'm the shortest person in the store yet I'm the one that has to clean the mirrors 10 feet above ground! Does this make sense to anyone?

juliet1318
17/F/United States

What is the worst work experience you've ever had?

Mezmer
18/F/United Kingdom

Q

A

Picking maggots outta rotten potatoes at a grocery store.

jewelz_52
18/F/United States

I was poodle-sitting for the next-door neighbors. I went to get the dog out of its kennel to take it for a walk . . . and it wasn't moving or breathing. It was dead. I called my neighbors on their cell phone and told them what happened. They rushed home, took one look at the dog, and started laughing at me. It turns out the dog had narcolepsy. I wanted to die.

kjbrat1203
16/F/United States

What's the craziest thing you've ever done for money?

hotangel_babe
16/F/United States

Q

A

Spit over the balcony in our state capitol onto some bald dude's head.

palinmalk
16/F/United States

Not the craziest, but the stupidest thing I've done is have sex. I was a heroin addict at the time and would have done anything for it. Not recommended.

Morgasm4
18/F/United States

You're arrested for murder and grand larceny by the Feds. They offer to cut you a deal that involves wearing a wire, but you're guaranteed a three-month sentence. What do you do?

lightofnight
17/F/United States

Q

A

I'd take the wire and throw it right back at them, then jump out the window before the whole building explodes from the bomb that my men planted while I was being questioned . . . escaping to my private jet that will take me away to Thailand until things cool down.

Xentric
17/F/United States

It depends on how long my sentence would be if I didn't take the deal, and who I'd be snooping on. If it's the big boss himself, hell no, 'cause he can just as easily snuff me out. I'd go to prison without the deal, but hey—do the crime, serve the time.

virgurl
19/F/United States

gettin' some

What did your first kiss feel like?

smiling_247
18/F/United States

Q

A

Dizzying, but really sweet.

SilverFaery
16/F/United States

All I remember is, it was with some guy, it didn't mean anything, and I didn't like it.

ShadySkank
15/F/United States

My first kiss was terrible. It was set up by the girl's friends. It had no emotion in it at all and was the worst experience ever.

universalfriend
19/M/United States

Does virginity really matter these days?

LouiseSutton
19/F/United Kingdom

Q

Some of my friends saw losing their virginity as a gateway into a world of promiscuous sex, while my virginity is important to me.

ala1993
20/M/United Kingdom

It's just the first time you have sex, for God's sake. You're gonna do it loads more, so what's the big deal?

Lilcockney
16/F/United Kingdom

You're caught masturbating by your mother. What now?

rubbertoe
19/M/Tuvalu

Q

A

Just pack up my shit and never look back.

rndy
17/M/United States

Start stabbing yourself with a pen to make her think you've lost it.

Mr._Spoon
15/M/United States

I'd tell her, "If you don't want to be surprised, don't surprise others."

PacificLight
20/F/United States

Name something your parents told you when you were little that you now know was a lie.

skurv
18/F/United States

Q

A

My mom told me my cat ran away, when actually she'd run it over.

1Candy3
15/F/United States

What worries you most about having sex?

boltpunk
22/M/United States

Q

A

That I'm going to regret it.

IM007
20/F/Netherlands

If a girl sleeps around, she's a slut, but if a guy sleeps around, people think he's cool. What do you think?

scammer
15/M/United Kingdom

A

Girls who sleep around are sluts. Guys that sleep around are sluts. Neither are cool.

Ossander
18/M/United States

That is the biggest double standard ever. If it's okay for guys then why is it not okay for girls? I'm not saying people should be promiscuous, but there should at least be the same set of rules for everyone.

FallenAngel_262
19/F/Canada

It has ruined my dating life 'cause nobody wants to date the slut, they just want to get with her and then leave her for the relationship type.

PRTTYGRL41115
15/F/United States

How long should you be in a relationship before it's okay to start having sex?

☐ *A day*
☐ *A week*
☐ *A month*
☐ *Six months*
☐ *A year*
☐ *Two years*
☐ *Three years or longer*
☐ *Until you're married*

DruidMoon
18/F/United States

A

A day: 5%
A week: 3%
A month: 22%
Six months: 22%
A year: 16%
Two years: 5%
Three years or longer: 2%
Until you're married: 25%

What would you do if your best friend came out to you?

abercrombie1066
16/M/United States

Personally, I would find it extremely uplifting because it would show how much my friend trusted me.

sk8rbert
16/M/United States

My best friend is homophobic. If she came out to me, I'd laugh my ass off.

CappucinoKitty
16/F/United States

Be sad . . . and support her.

rasberryswirl
18/F/United States

If you could arrange the perfect setting for sex, where would it be?

rafiki_tikigod
19/M/United States

Q

In a punk's bedroom. There would be posters on the walls, toy soldiers, and action figures all over the floor, a bass guitar in the corner of room. The TV would be on. His bed is a mattress on the floor with blue sheets and comforters that a 10-year-old would have.

CasperVixBuni3
15/F/United States

A

During a thunderstorm in a graveyard. I know it might sound sick, but that's me.

kdkid
23/M/United States

I'm not into that whole "the entire perfect night with a perfect dinner" and whatnot. For me, it would be for us to be alone at his house, watching TV under the covers with the rain pounding on the windows. We would turn to each other and feel the warmth in each other's eyes and know.

Nirvana_Fan
16/F/United States

In the elevator at the mall.

shit_for_brains
15/F/United States

What do you think about interracial dating?

trackbarbie
15/F/United States

Q

A

Well, I'm biracial so no matter who I'm dating it's interracial. I'm all for it!

keelynr1
17/F/United States

I'm extremely against it. I'm not in any way racist and I don't believe any race is better than another. I just believe God put us here as separate races on purpose, and it is very wrong to mix them. I'm not saying races shouldn't be friends, but anything further should not happen.

kelly715
15/F/United States

Love is love.

SonicChild
22/M/United States

When do you start getting possessive in a relationship?

Knox444
20/M/United Kingdom

Q

A

After I have sex with a guy, all hell breaks loose! I start having doubts and keep thinking he's cheating on me.

sexkitten_y2k
19/F/United States

I am completely possessive from the moment I club a guy over the head with a boot to the moment he is bound and gagged in my basement, sustained on King Vitamin cereal and Kool-Aid. If he even dares to scream for help, I subject him to hours of taped episodes of "America's Funniest Home Videos." "Hey! Shut your mouth!"

phlegmbouyant
21/F/United States

What do you find most irresistible about a person?

orangepuff
18/F/United States

Q

A

I like girls who smile wide and laugh without trying to contain it. I dunno why.

JetsetLounge568
15/M/United States

I like punk boys with little bellies—not fat boys, just little bellies.

vandalgrrl
19/F/United States

Thick eyebrows! Hell yeah, it's like, "Whoa!"

lyn-lyn1186
17/F/United States

Why get married?

NikkiNoNics
18/F/England

Q

Spouses are tax-deductible.

Madme
17/F/England

My question exactly. What's the point? If you want to be with someone forever, you don't need a piece of paper to prove it.

genisse
19/F/United Kingdom

A

Why not get married? If you love someone enough that you want to spend the rest of your life with them, then by all means go ahead. It's better than being single at age 60.

Anaardvark
19/M/United Kingdom

Security and love.

hollywood_sux
16/M/United Kingdom

So you can have really good sex on tap.

joanne4503
16/F/United Kingdom

Is it okay to cheat?

SableMoon84
16/F/Canada

Q

You should do whatever your heart tells you. Just one piece of advice: You'll regret cheating. I know from experience.

Elizabeth4856
15/F/United States

Hell no. Keep it in your pants, champ.

free_kidneys
16/M/Australia

If you're a girl, it's okay to cheat. If you're a guy, it's not. At least, that's what girls believe. And they get to call the shots.

PunkRockBoy
17/M/United States

What's the cruelest way you've ever dumped someone?

Subira
17/F/United States

Q

A

I tried over and over to tell this one guy nicely, but he just didn't get it. . . . So I called a local radio station that I knew was always on at his house and announced that I didn't like him anymore and that it was over.

ILoVeJoNdAvIs69
15/F/United States

My boyfriend cheated on me, so I told him that I was dumping him for his sister 'cause she was better in bed—just to see the look on his face!

TaStle69
19/F/United States

How can you tell you're in love?

princess_3879
19/F/United States

Q

A

When you don't notice your crush's hot cousin.

achickthatkix
17/F/United States

When you really hurt a lot.

whyynott
19/M/United States

When you can honestly picture the two of you 50 years old and still married.

andarial
17/F/United States

I think love is that can't-eat, can't-sleep, reach-for-the-stars, over-the-fence, World Series kinda feeling.

Mitsey
15/F/United States

Why would chicks rather stay with jerks than go out with nice guys?

goatman118
19/M/United States

Q

It's not that ladies prefer jerks, it's just the way it happens. Before you go out, he's really nice to you, and by the time you realize your mistake, you're tangled in the brambles and can't get out that easily.

jellibean6215
16/F/United States

A

I am uncomfortable with guys who are completely nice because in my experience they turn out to be gay and we wind up just being friends.

TrinityBlaze
15/F/United States

I've never gone out with a jerk. "Jerks" are not "hot" because they put out "jerk rays" which makes them unrad.

supereyeball
18/F/United States

Jerks are more interesting. There's more fun in those relationships. I feel bad when I'm with a total sweetheart—I feel undeserving of the attention and guilty for liking it.

powerpuffpunk
17/F/United States

What's the dumbest thing you've done to show off for a guy or a girl?

alternarock83
17/F/United States

Q

A

I was trying to be all smooth and put my arm around this girl. I accidentally elbowed her and gave her a black eye instead!

cOdex
17/M/United States

You know how some girls can tie a cherry stem into a knot with their tongue? Well, I told my boyfriend I could do that, although I had never even tried to before, and I choked on the stem. He still teases me about it.

punkskunz
17/F/United States

Me and a friend of mine once got into a fake fight to impress a girl. Unfortunately for us, the school supervisor was also watching. But when the dean of students heard our story—we told the truth—he started cracking up. We still got suspended, though.

SquirrelMan492
17/M/United States

What's the best way to end a first date?

supagirlie
20/F/United Kingdom

A

Go to Denny's. Steal forks, knives, and ashtrays, then exit through the bathroom window. After that, go to a park, whip up a fire, cook marshmallows, and go hunting for pigeons with superglue on our fingertips.

180toafaceplant
19/M/United States

who to eat and what to wear

If you were in a plane crash and had to eat a famous person, who would it be and why?

Homunculus777
17/M/United States

Q

A

I would eat Dom DeLuise because he would be tender, yet meaty.

Patroclus
18/M/United States

Well, if I wanted to survive for at least a month, I would eat Jennifer Lopez, because there is enough "fat" in her butt to feed all the survivors.

muchachotierno
17/M/Canada

That would have to be Arnold Schwarzenwhatever. First, because I hate him. Second, because he's got all that muscle-meat to last as long as I need.

Js_Punkin
21/F/United States

What was the most dangerous toy you had growing up?

lilbutrcup
22/F/United States

Q

A

My Barbies, believe it or not. I used to melt them and cut off their hair and hang their heads from my ceiling. I hated Barbie 'cause she had things I didn't have. Somewhere at my grandma's house there's a pile of flesh-colored goo to prove it.

sc_kat
16/F/United States

My neighbor's potato gun.

aaron_mm
16/M/United States

What is the most annoying fashion trend?

stimey
16/F/United States

Q

A

SKIRTS OVER TROUSERS! I just don't get it! It's like wearing two T-shirts! Another stupid fashion statement!

> *sirspankypants*
> *16/M/United Kingdom*

Wearing pants below your ass. . . .

> *violetsky95*
> *23/F/United States*

Capri pants are the ugliest things I've ever seen in my life.

> *BananaRepubGurl*
> *16/F/United States*

The glitter thing is SO played. I see girls with glitter over their eyes, on their arms, shoulders, in their hair! That has got to go!

> *YummiT*
> *17/F/United States*

If you could have a portal into anyone's brain, whose would it be? Think "Being John Malkovich."

LoLiEpOpPe
17/F/United States

Q

A

I would get into my friends' heads so I could find out what they really think of me.

Kitty_luvns
15/F/United States

Any woman's. Just to know how the opposite sex works for once, dammit!

falling_boy
21/M/United States

I would probably choose Hitler to see if he actually bought all the crap and propaganda he was spewing. I'd try to understand just why he did this awful stuff.

mer_de_noms29
18/M/United States

Name any porn star.

Wiccan_SunGod
16/M/United States

What would you do if you were able to jump inside your TV?

punkassjuggalo
16/F/Canada

Q

A

I'd kill Kenny.

vampiresmile
17/F/United States

I would step into "Who Wants to Be a Millionaire?" and tell Regis to cut the dramatic crap and just say whether the answer is right or wrong.

sibtiger15
15/F/United States

What's the worst movie ever?

evilgoddess01
17/F/United States

Q

"Spice World" [shivers].

KinderwhoreE
18/F/Canada

Don't bitch until you've seen "The Perfect Storm." It was just waves and a boat for two and a half hours.

blondy_prncz038
15/F/United States

"Return of the Killer Tomatoes" . . . pass the vomit bag please.

Vampirize
22/M/Canada

"E.T." – it gives me nightmares.

blackcherrysky
16/F/United States

"Lake Placid." Dude, I was just happy the cow lived! And I do not plan to see another screwed-up animal movie! They all suck—"Bats" sucked and "Anaconda" sucked!

K2Sk8erGirl
16/F/United States

"Fargo"! GGGRRRRRR, that movie sucks—we North Dakotans don't talk like that.

Babygirlj7
18/F/United States

A

If you could fight any celebrity, who would it be and why?

☐ *William Shatner*
☐ *Dick Clark*
☐ *Meatloaf*
☐ *Gandhi*
☐ *Other*

ChodaBoy
17/M/United States

Q

William Shatner: 2%
Dick Clark: 1%
Meatloaf: 2%
Gandhi: 1%
Other: 94%

A

Living or dead? Dead, I'd have to say Hitler. Living, maybe Mr. T. I'd get my ass kicked, but that's okay 'cause he's hella tough.

MadMike22
17/M/United States

I think I'd take on Estelle Getty from "Golden Girls," because I'm not very tough, and I think I could take on an elderly woman.

Sigur_Ros
19/M/Australia

I'd have to go along with everyone else and say Britney Spears.

wwf_mosh_chic
18/F/United States

Dick Clark—I'll make that bastard age!

Duk144
15/M/United States

What's the perfect band to listen to while venting your rage?

Liquid22
17/M/United States

Q

A

Slipknot

Pimp-Mama1
16/F/United States

Cannibal Corpse

MISFIT2000
15/M/United States

Korn

g3ck03
15/F/United States

DJ Spooky

little_deviant
19/F/United States

Offspring

DrNickPhD
17/M/United States

Atari Teenage Riot

Succubus56
18/F/United States

Limp Bizkit

Lizard_Queen17
18/F/Australia

What's the worst song of all time?

cRazEe-aSsbITcH
16/F/United States

Q

"MMM Bop" by Hanson. They introduced us to a new level of talentless drivel, somehow put under the category of a song. The music is discordant and choppy, the lyrics are insipid, and hell, they sound like chicks.

Carebin
15/F/Canada

Any song by Britney "breast implant" Spears.

playboy_4122
15/M/United States

I'd have to say it's a tie between "Big Pimpin'" and "The Thong Song." I know that I'm just about the only one who thinks so, but all these stupid pathetic loser guys have made those their theme songs, and it's so irritating!

starausty
15/F/United States

What book, song, or movie makes you cry?

XxREBELxX
17/F/New Zealand

A

"Where Is My Mind?" by the Pixies, because my friend who died loved that song, and it makes me think of him.

> *619chic*
> *17/F/United States*

"Night" by Elie Wiesel.

> *J-China*
> *15/F/United States*

The only movie that's done it to me has been "Saving Private Ryan." Not the ending so much as the very beginning. To see people doing that to each other is pretty traumatic.

> *DaddyPants*
> *18/M/United States*

What is your favorite movie quote?

austin1648
18/F/United States

Q

A

"You like apples? I got her number. How do you like them apples?" from "Good Will Hunting"

Meredith_613
16/F/United States

"Say my name, bitch!" from "American Pie"

SpAceChIC1329
16/F/United States

"You don't want to get mixed up with a guy like me. I'm a loner, Dottie. A rebel," from "Pee Wee's Big Adventure"

Jamie_monet
15/M/United States

"Does Barry Manilow know you raid his wardrobe?" from "The Breakfast Club"

ella03
19/F/United States

If you could make a movie about anything, what would it be about?

titicaca80
20/F/United States

Q

It would probably have to do with a giant peanut that crashed into Earth. Ends up that the peanut is really a spaceship, and inside are aliens that look like koalas. Unlike koalas, however, they devour human flesh.

golux
17/M/United States

I'm already making a musical about pigeons called "Pidge: The First Cut."

titicaca80
20/F/United States

Killer monkeys from the center of the Earth.

sublim1357
16/M/United States

I would make a movie about suicide—people who have tried it, why they tried it, or why they didn't, what their lives are like now, how the choices they made affected the people around them. Or, I would make a movie about a marching band.

Indie_Simon
16/F/United States

It would be a group of four kats runnin' the spot in their neighborhood. Blowin' trees, drinkin', gettin' with mad girls, livin' large, drivin' Range Rovers, and gettin' into drama. But instead of them all dying in the end like most movies, they would get up out the drama and retire on the low low.

Face2Face124
17/M/United States

I'd have the book "The Catcher in the Rye" made into a movie . . . with a bangin' guy as the lead.

StarGazer622
15/F/United States

Do you think fashion magazines are inspiring or depressing?

flipgirl182
17/F/Canada

I hate how image is so important. Who decides what is beautiful and special? A magazine? That makes me really sad.

lost_etc
21/F/United States

A

I love fashion magazines. I admit I am slim and tall. I'm also a guy—a gay guy. And I love designer clothes. Magazines give you tips on what's hot and what's not. If you don't like them, you're free not to read them.

kweenbryan
18/M/Philippines

I don't think girls should judge their looks against models with eating disorders. I don't know any guys who like super-skeletal girls anyway.

nrub
16/M/United States

If you let them get to you, they can be depressing. Sometimes I wish my makeup would look that good, my hair would be curly, or my body would be that perfect. I try not to read them anymore.

mys_star
17/F/Canada

What's your policy on plastic surgery?

☐ *If you want to look better, it's a must.*
☐ *Only for medical purposes.*
☐ *Nobody should ever have it done.*

joshleeper
18/M/United States

Q

A

If you want to look better, it's a must. 32%
Only for medical purposes. 68%
Nobody should ever have it done. 0%

What do you think of upper-class white kids imitating and adopting black hip-hop culture?

Q

hardrock5439
15/M/United States

I think people should be allowed to be different without being criticized for it. Nobody has the right to say what kind of music a person can listen to based on the color of their skin or how rich or preppy they are.

freaky_psyco
15/F/United States

They all need to be slapped upside the head. Whenever I'm driving and I see someone like that, I always have to roll down my window and yell, "You're white!"

pinkmoon484
16/F/United States

The music industry has long been the outlet for "rebellion" against parents, but now the generation that rebelled with rock is the establishment. So now, the record companies sell rap as a way to rebel. And by buying into it, you're actually conforming, not rebelling. It happens with every generation.

DaddyPants
18/M/United States

What is your favorite thing from the '80s?

writer_chic_15
16/F/Canada

Q

A

The style and the music. Kill me and reincarnate me as an '80s chickamaroo. Please.

laterskater
17/F/United States

"Degrassi High"

crazychristian
22/F/Australia

Atari, real Nintendo (not Super Nintendo or any of that other crap), "Bill and Ted's Excellent Adventure," and this bag I had with a unicorn on it.

snorkle
17/F/United States

Garbage Pail Kids, "Fraggle Rock," Rainbow Brite. Ahhh, those were the days!

shadylady2000
16/F/United Kingdom

life, death, and the big lie

What song would you want to have played at your funeral?

Amy9653
20/F/United States

Q

A

"Baby Got Back" by Sir Mix-A-Lot. It's a mood lifter.

Sungoddess_88
17/F/United States

What happens to us when we die?

maddgrrl
16/F/Canada

Q

A

We decompose. That's it. Show me some proof to the contrary. And, frankly, who cares? You've got a good 80 years to get done whatever you need to get done. Get to work.

Blotman_X
17/M/Canada

I don't believe my grandmother is just underground decomposing. I think she's happy in heaven with God.

sweetpea5288
18/F/United States

I'm gonna be a ghost and scare people.

MetalHeadGrrl
17/F/United States

What would you do if you found out your best friend had killed his or her family?

PaleSpiral
17/F/United States

Q

A

I'd wonder why at first. My best friend has a really nice family and he seems to like them a lot. But if he had a good reason to kill them, I'd leave with him.

ybagirl
16/F/United States

I'd help her hide the bodies.

BloodOfAReptile
19/F/United States

I would turn her in before she turned on me.

dielwi
17/F/Canada

If you created your own religion, what would be the biggest sin?

vic...
18/M/United States

Q

A

Using a screen name incorporating "QT" or "sexy" or "hot" (various spellings of the aforementioned included).

AnarchistCow123
15/F/United States

Not having sex!

SexyLatino921
17/M/United States

Not wearing deodorant and not brushing your teeth. Being smelly in general.

prodigyfire
16/M/United States

Having a mullet.

writer_chic_15
16/F/Canada

I'm playing God today. I have decided that you can have one of the following people back on Earth. Pick one:

☐ *Jimi Hendrix*
☐ *River Phoenix*
☐ *Jim Morrison*
☐ *Brandon Lee*
☐ *Chris Farley*

SaraXXXAngel
20/F/United States

Q

A

Jimi Hendrix: 33%
River Phoenix: 14%
Jim Morrison: 19%
Brandon Lee: 9%
Chris Farley: 25%

River Phoenix, because he is fine and he would be so grateful to me for bringing him back to life he would HAVE to go out with me!

lizajaneuk
18/F/United Kingdom

Chris Farley! We need real comedians, because Adam Sandler blows.

DeViLzAngeL1701
17/F/United States

Do you have a personal relationship with God?

stoutamire25
18/M/United States

Q

I think I do. Recently my 17-day-old brother died, and God's helped me be strong and survive.

kissandtell19
18/F/United States

We talk, yes. I think there's a budding friendship there, but we don't have a "personal relationship" yet.

cloud9spaz
16/F/United States

A

Other than still being pissed off at Him for killing my mom, no.

crazy_chick2343
15/F/United States

I stay out of His business, He stays out of mine.

RiotPoofGrrrl
15/F/United States

Yep. She's having my baby, actually.

RavenDigger
17/M/Canada

Yes, I do, but I had a better one before I started questioning and examining my religious beliefs.

shehavoc
17/F/United States

Do you have a lucky charm?

LuckyDuck32
18/F/United States

Q

A

I always carry around the severed ear of my favorite baby toy, Mr. Snuggles. My sister ruined the rest, and all I saved was the ear. It makes me feel better to have it.

ybagirl
16/F/United States

It's this horse pin that my grandma gave me. The pin part broke off, but I keep the horse in my purse and it protects me wherever I go.

AlienHead7583
17/F/United States

Yep—my cross that's made out of bloodstone. I try to wear it at all times and don't let anybody touch it.

Gahlta
16/F/Australia

What's the nicest thing you've done for someone you didn't know?

q_berter
20/M/United States

Q

A

I was at a football game, and I helped a three-year-old find his mother.

poet_17
15/F/United States

I saved a drunk 14-year-old girl from drowning this summer. The thanks I got? Her mother cursing me out for bringing her back like that. What was I supposed to do? I didn't even know her, but I couldn't just let her drown.

Iamfreespirited
19/F/Canada

I helped build a homeless dude's house!

Signal64
17/M/United States

What's the best way to get revenge on somebody?

**PaleSpiral
17/F/United States**

Q

A

Hide seafood in their car. They will never get the smell out.

Nauticastud
18/M/United States

What's the biggest lie you've ever told?

ollieplimsoll
22/M/Wales

Q

A

I told my parents I wasn't gay. But they found out. Let's just say it didn't go over well.

DepressedKitten
17/M/United States

I said I was a 65-year-old guy on the Internet.

BeachBaby345
16/F/United States

I told my girlfriend that I still loved her.

BEATDOCKTA
24/M/United States

If you knew that your friend's boyfriend or girlfriend had cheated on them, would you tell your friend?

KristenL
16/F/Canada

Q

I would talk to the cheater about confessing, but if they didn't want to, I wouldn't tell, 'cause it's none of my business.

twigy15
15/F/United States

When I was in the seventh grade, I found out certain things that led me to believe my father was cheating on my mother. I never told her because I couldn't see what good would come of it. I would tell a friend that their boyfriend was cheating, though, because I'm closer to my friends than to my family.

IcyLuna
18/F/United States

Should the war on drugs be ended?

SnaKeChArmer187
15/M/United States

Q

A

War? It's more like a politically correct protest started by the government.

Kittie667
17/F/United States

Wait a minute, I thought drugs won the war years ago.

SonicChild
21/M/United States

No. We see enough people getting hooked on drugs and ruining their lives. I don't need to see any more idiots walking around the hallways at school. Weed isn't that bad, but we need to keep fighting to get rid of all the other stuff.

JaksWastedLife
15/F/United States

What is the worst thing you have ever done?

BaByJaWs
15/F/United States

Q

*I was at the mall with two friends and we were really bored, but very hyper.
Being the twisted psychopaths we are, we ran around the whole mall naked
singing our favorite song, "What's My Age Again?" We got caught by a security
guard, had to spend four weeks in juvenile detention, had to pay a $2,400 fine,
and I'm still grounded.*

gimpy27_03
15/M/United States

A

I beat the crap out of my best friend because he took my PlayStation.

lethal-killa
15/M/United States

*We broke into my neighbor's house when they were out of town. We totally
rearranged the furniture. When they got back they totally freaked.*

madnWild
16/M/United States

*A group of friends and I decided to play a prank on my best friend. Earlier that
day I had "borrowed" a roll of shrink-wrap from work. We wrapped his car up
with the whole roll. You couldn't see the car at all—just a big gob of plastic
wrap. Anyway, it took him about 45 minutes to unwrap it the next morning.
That was three years ago and he still has no idea who did it.*

tendtherabbits
19/M/United States

*I told a guy at a party I was gay to get rid of him, then made out with his older
brother right in front of him.*

littleqt313
15/F/United States

How do you feel about animal testing?

mystic_orca
18/F/Canada

Q

A

It's okay if it's just on rats, mice, and snakes. Those animals suck!

CuteCheerChic04
15/F/United States

It's absolutely not okay to do it for things like perfume and cosmetics. That's crazy. I think it's okay for life-saving drugs, though. What if it were you or someone you loved who might die without those drugs?

subnivean
17/F/Canada

You're about to be in a car accident. If you swerve to the left you will hit another car head-on and be seriously injured. If you swerve to the right, you'll hit and kill a pedestrian. Which would you do?

☐ *Swerve to the left and be seriously injured*
☐ *Swerve to the right and kill some innocent person*

k_moneymoney
17/F/United States

Q

A

Swerve to the left and be seriously injured: 77%
Swerve to the right and kill some innocent person: 23%

Think of someone you absolutely despise. If you had their life in your hands, would you kill them?

Lady_Cyrania
15/F/United States

Q

No, but if they needed rescuing and rescuing them would put my life in danger, I'd risk it because then they would be indebted to me and if I died, they would feel eternally guilty.

A_Ramsell
18/F/United States

A

No, although I almost killed my little brother last summer. I didn't mean to—I just kind of cut off his oxygen supply for about a minute. Ever since then, he's been really scared of me. I hate the look in his eyes and I'm so sorry I ever did it, even though he did really tick me off.

btrfly_85
15/F/United States

Yes. I would strangle them with their own tongue.

Malystrx
21/M/United States

Oh yes! I would torture them first while making them watch "Barney." I would start with their feet and work my way up, purposely missing the vital organs.

WesFreak666
15/F/United States

If you bumped a car in a parking lot and no one saw you do it, would you leave a note?

Clayrivoyance
19/F/United States

Q

A

What bump?

jast187
16/M/United States

The best way to die would be. . .

☐ *Freezing*
☐ *Burning*
☐ *Being shot in the head*
☐ *Strangulation*
☐ *Drowning*
☐ *Getting smacked over the head with a two-by-four*
☐ *Falling off a cliff*
☐ *Being eaten by a shark*
☐ *Amusement park accident*
☐ *Head-on collision while getting oral sex*

maddgrrl
16/F/Canada

Q

A

Freezing: 7%
Burning: 5%
Being shot in the head: 17%
Strangulation: 2%
Drowning: 9%
Getting smacked over the head with a two-by-four: 2%
Falling off a cliff: 9%
Being eaten by a shark: 9%
Amusement park accident: 6%
Head-on collision while getting oral sex: 34%

Tagbook questions are only the beginning. Find out what more than 4 million Bolt members around the world already know: Bolt hooks you up with ways to speak your mind, meet people, and get down with free email, clubs, Bolt Notes, homepages, and more. Still need convincing? Here's what a few Bolt members had to say:

I love Bolt so much—if I could have sex with it, I would. I don't know what I did with my free time before Bolt.

sallysallysally
16/F/United States

I live on Bolt—it's my home. My dog's name is Bolt.

Scorpion_77
22/M/South Africa

The first day I was on Bolt, I made three friends in about an hour. I'm a shy person, so that normally doesn't happen for me.

Freshman_20
19/M/United States

Check out **www.bolt.com** and see what they're talking about.

America Online Keyword: Bolt

About the Editors

Dennis Sarkozy (Bolt name: ruse) attends high school in New Jersey. He believes strongly in animal rights and a straight-edge lifestyle and enjoys learning about other people's cultures and religions.

Kate Levitt (Bolt name: Kwalaty) is a student at Columbia University and is originally from San Francisco. In her spare time, she likes to DJ, break-dance, and write.

Michael Gartland (Bolt name: sauvier) is a senior channel manager at Bolt. When he isn't cooking up ideas there, he's either writing, reading, or exploring New York City's vast tunnel system.

Ari Voukydis (Bolt name: ari007) is the editor of Bolt. He is also a writer, actor, and comedian who's appeared on NBC's "Late Night With Conan O'Brien."

Elizabeth Hurchalla (Bolt name: Lissa) is the senior content director at Bolt. She spent her teen years in Wayne, Pennsylvania, where she enjoyed selling popcorn at the Budco Gateway Cinema and hanging out at the King of Prussia Mall.